Till Ink Meets Paper:
Poems For Guendalina…My Mommy

By Jose Angel Perez

'Till Ink Meets Paper

POEMS FOR GUENDALINA...
MY MOMMY

'Till Ink Meets Paper: Poems for Guendalina…My Mommy

Written by Jose Angel Perez

Copyright © 2024 by Jose Angel Perez. All rights reserved.

No part of this publication may be reproduced, distributed, or transmitted in any form or by any means, including photocopying, recording, or other electronic or mechanical methods, without the prior written permission of the author, except in the case of brief quotations embodied in critical reviews and certain other non-commercial uses permitted by copyright law. For permission requests, contact the author at jperez.poetry@gmail.com

This is a work of poetry. Names, characters, places, and incidents are rooted in true events, entirely drawn from the author's personal experiences. Any similarities to other stories or characters are purely coincidental.

First Edition

Printed in United States of America
ISBN: 979-8-9856777-8-2

Cover Design by Jose A. Perez

For inquiries, readings, speaking events, performances, or additional copies please email the author at jperez.poetry@gmail.com

To Beia
My Beautiful Powerful Princess

For Mommy
Guendalina "Wendy" Ruberte
Rest in Power, Mommy
I got You!

Mommy,

You came to me on purpose
with your nurturing touch,
loving me with what you know,
In a world surrounded by steel and bars
you knew what to do.

In shadows deep where silence reigns,
A mother's love broke through my chains.
Her lullabies, a whispered song,
In ink and paper, where we belong.
Though systems seized, they couldn't take
The bond we forged, the dreams we made.
Her art, a bridge from her to me,
In every line, her spirit is free.
For justice, humanity, peace I seek,
In words, she lives; in love, we speak.

Till Ink Meets Paper,

Love Your Son

Dear Reader...Yes You...My Brother, My Sister

Self-Care is important before you read this book! *Till Ink Meets Paper: Poems for Guendalina...My Mommy* captures the essence of my mother's love, a stark contrast to the painful separation imposed on us by the child welfare system. Before you embark on this journey through my words, I gently encourage you to nurture yourself in the ways that resonate with your heart. Each of us walks our own path of self-care, and I want to remind you that these poems may stir feelings within you. If you've known the heartache of having a loved one behind bars, lose someone you care about, or if your journey has taken you through the foster care system, you might find echoes of your own story within these lines.

I invite you to embrace whatever emotions arise—be they sorrow, anger, or a tender longing—especially if they lead you to unhealed wounds. Your feelings are valid, and it's important to honor them. Engage in the healing practices that speak to you, whether through reflection, art, or connection with others.

As you read, know that it's perfectly okay to step back if you feel overwhelmed. You are not alone in this space; your worthiness of love, healing, and joy is profound. I hold your well-being in my thoughts, and I hope these poems can offer you a moment of grace, perhaps even towards those with whom you may feel resentment.

Remember, you are a precious being, deserving of kindness—both from others and yourself. Your journey matters, and you are cherished.

Why these Particular Poems?

The foster care agency shattered my bond with my mother when I was just three years old, igniting a storm of worthlessness, hopelessness, and rage within me. This agency, failing to support my mother in her rightful role, left my family adrift, as I bounced from home to home until eventually I found myself on Rikers Island. My mother, too, was imprisoned there, a heartbreaking testament to a system that should have nurtured us but instead condemned us. We found ourselves in the darkest corners of New York City—a mother and her child, confined in separate cells on the same island. How could this have happened?

This was the inevitable result of a family under the watchful eye of a government agency that failed us at every turn. In the year 2002, although in prison, my mother and I managed to rekindle something between us. We exchanged letters and poetry while imprisoned on Rikers Island, our words swirling into our cells like leaves in a storm.

Here we were, a mother and son trapped in one of New York City's darkest corners.

Growing up in foster care and later as a teenage inmate, I whispered a vow into the void: "My first published collection of poetry will be for my mom." Years apart bred deep resentment, and I used to blame my mother for all of it. Why didn't she want me? What didn't she fight for me. The truth is that she did fight for me. But she was a byproduct of systems that failed to protect us. The foster care system, masquerading as a lifeline, uprooted me and my siblings under the guise of opportunity, yet delivered us to institutions that stripped away our humanity.

I was taken away from her at 3 years old, and placed with other families that were supposed to be better than my mother's care, better than her nurturing, better than her effort. Yet, there is not one adult who can claim success in their mission to protect me. Instead, they funneled us into a cycle of neglect and despair, replacing nurturing homes with over-surveilled environments that literally mirror prison life.

The Children's Village for example, gave us pillows, sheets, and mattresses that mirrored that of the prison systems. The Corcraft brand, a textile multi-million-dollar enterprise that uses prisoners to produce their products. The very same products that are in all of your public schools, government agencies and in your child welfare institutions to name a few. The resemblance is not just shocking—it's a damning indictment of a system designed to fail. It endangers the very children it claims to save. I lived in carceral environments due to the government deeming my mother an unfit mother, terminating her parental rights due to her own carceral experience and she suffered from gang culture and substance abuse. My mother needed nurturing. I needed nurturing. Yet the punishment for being someone in need, someone poor, someone without resources to uplift themselves, is more abuse and neglect from a government that has the power to label people as they deem unfit.

Enough.

It is time to tell the truth about my mother. She was Love. She was Amazing. She needed a little extra help to get her bearings together as a mom, she needed people. She needed community. She needed Grace. The arrogance of the New York government to deem someone unfit, uproot children from their family as a result of this label, then placed them in a system that has the worst possible outcomes for human beings–especially young girls and boys who look just like me.

Through this collection, I aspire to uplift my mother, to bring her the justice, humanity, and peace she so richly deserves after having me and my siblings torn from her arms by the child welfare system.

My mother, Guendalina, was ensnared by systems designed to perpetuate her struggles—systems steeped in colonial roots that denied her the nurturing care essential to her role as a mother. Even while we shared the confines of Rikers Island, she found solace in writing love letters and poetry. Those words became her lifeline, a testament to her fierce spirit as she battled the demons of addiction and gang culture. The system used her hardships as justification to label her unfit, stripping her of dignity, hope, and respect.

This collection serves as my public acknowledgment of Guendalina Ruberte's humanity. She was a mother like any other, her love radiating through her unique expressions. Her fierce affection, captured in every letter, proves that love can flourish even in the darkest corners of despair. My mother's spirit endures through the art I present to you. If you believe in that magic, as I do, my poetry becomes the love language she instilled in me, guiding me through life's storms, especially during our time on Rikers Island.

In the desolate confines of incarceration, where shadows of an uncertain future loom long and hope flickers like a fragile candle in the wind, my mother emerged as a steadfast beacon, nurturing my passion for poetry when my spirit felt most fragile. Each letter she penned was a lifeline, a delicate thread woven with love and resilience, bridging the vast chasm that separated us. Yet, years later, the cruel machinery of the system laid bare its ruthless intent: when prison guards seized my mother's letters, it became painfully clear how they sought to sever the sacred bonds of family. The correctional officers at Clinton Correctional Facility, in their cold indifference, echoed the oppressive forces that had sought to erase my spirit since I was just three years old. They obliterated not only her words but also the cherished remnants of our shared dreams—photos of sunlit days, verses that whispered of hope, some of which I, in a tempest of anger, cast aside.

But amid the ruins of those stolen moments, I unearthed within myself a flicker of defiance. From the ashes of despair, I forged a fierce resolve, transforming pain into purpose. I became a poet because of my mother, each verse a testament to our unbreakable bond, a reflection of our intertwined souls. I began to weave my own words anew, crafting a path toward liberation, where every line I wrote became a rebellion against silence, an anthem for all hearts bound by walls yet yearning for freedom. I aspired to embody my poetry, for in it I could envision immortality—the reverence of words and the taste of freedom mingling in a tangible dance, a celebration of resilience that would echo through the corridors of time.

As a 17-year-old prisoner at Clinton Correctional Facility, I embarked on a mission to write. I created my first unpublished work, The Walls of a Gray Cloud. This collection will feature those raw, unedited poems—fragmented with misspellings and imperfections—as a gift to you, a glimpse into the mind of a teenager navigating life within one of the country's most dangerous men's maximum-security prisons: Clinton Correctional Facility.

The poems you are about to read are the echoes of my journey, weaving together the tapestry of my experiences, fears, and hopes—essential threads in the fabric of my survival. Two decades later, I emerged as a voice for young souls like mine, evolving into a child wellbeing advocate, standing tall within the embrace of The Children's Defense Fund-New York, the largest child welfare non-profit in the nation, where I serve today as their Program Strategist. As I write these words in the Maya Angelou reading room at the Langston Hughes Library in Clinton, Tennessee, I sit at the Alex Haley Farm—a sanctuary for the Children's Defense Fund's alumni and current advocates, each one a beacon of hope across America.

As a former teenage lifer, I left the prison walls behind after 20 years, reborn as an actor, poet, and multi-disciplinary artist. When Parole granted me release in January 2024, it marked the first time in over 36 years that I was unshackled from the New York State government system.

Now, at 39, I stand before you, not just as a survivor, but as a testament to vulnerability mixed with power and a desire to take action, resilient even. Though I often bristle at that word. To label someone 'resilient' sometimes feels like an invitation for the world to heap even more burdens upon their shoulders. "Oh, he's strong; he can handle it," they say, but let me be clear: I am not your punching bag!

The child welfare system, which was meant to cradle me into being, was supposed to nurture my growth with love, compassion, and patience. Instead, it often felt like a cage, stifling my spirit rather than setting it free.

Yet from this tumult, I have emerged, determined to transform pain into purpose, to advocate for those who still fight to be seen and heard, lighting the way for others lost in the shadows. Especially Guendalina "Wendy" Ruberte–My Mommy.

Till Ink Meets Paper captures the essence of this transformative journey, illustrating how the seeds of creativity sown by my mother flourished even in oppressive environments. My mother's story, our story, is both an indictment of the child welfare system and a celebration of resilience, connection, hope, and community. I hope it resonates deeply with all who hear it. In every line I write, I strive to elevate my mother's power, restore her humanity, and honor the love that binds us forever.

The Year 2002

    The price of this collection holds deep significance for me. It symbolizes the year my mother and I embarked on a transformative journey to heal the fractures in our relationship—wounds that were carved by the unforgiving hands of the foster care system in New York City. Each word and poem reflect the resilience we summoned to navigate our pain, as we sought to mend the bonds that had been tested by circumstance.

    This collection is not just a price; it's a testament to our shared struggle, our growth, and our unwavering hope. It represents the strength we discovered within ourselves and each other as we reclaimed our narrative, turning hurt into healing. In every poem, you'll find echoes of our love—a love that endured through the trials, illuminating the path toward reconciliation and understanding. It is a powerful reminder that even the deepest wounds can be transformed into stories of triumph and grace.

A portion of the proceeds from this book will go toward honoring my mother's memory in a way that truly reflects her spirit. She rests in Puerto Rico, buried without a name—just a number on a cold stone. It is my heartfelt wish to provide her with a headstone that bears her name, a rightful acknowledgment of her life and the love she shared.

16 Poems

I share with you 16 poems, a reflection of the age when I first faced the walls of prison, and the age when my mother and I began to heal our bond. These words are a tribute to her, yet they also belong to you—those who yearn to witness how the connection between a mother and child can blossom, even in adversity.

The child welfare system often claims the mantle of care, stepping in when parents struggle with the weight of circumstance. But what stories emerge when we look beyond the labels? Where is the community support that helps families reclaim their strength? Where are the lessons, the grace, for those who seem lost, yet deserve our compassion? When we sever the ties between parents and their children, we deny the warmth of love and nurture that every child deserves.

Foster care children experience layers of erasure at every age, seeking answers to the silence of stability. We crave a home, a family—someone to say, "I love you," and to show it through action. Those three words are a promise, a lifeline.

These 16 poems emerge from a time when my anger and feelings of worthlessness swelled within me, shaped by a system that cast me adrift. I felt the ache of loss—my mother's rights stripped away, our family bonds frayed.

The Walls of A Gray Cloud

Yet from this struggle, creativity blossomed, nourished by the unwavering love of my mother. After I was sentenced to 20 years to life, I was sent upstate to serve what felt like an eternity. It was in that isolation, shaped by the deep longing for connection, that I found my voice. My mother sent me letters, encouraging me to respond with my own words, embedding within me a sense of discipline and artistry.

Each letter was a lifeline, a reminder that our bond could transcend the prison walls that sought to confine me. As I poured my thoughts onto the page, what emerged was an unpublished collection of poems I titled *The Walls of a Gray Cloud*. These poems became the seeds of vulnerability and power, the very essence of my survival.

They captured the tumult of my emotions and the longing for the nurturing love we had once shared, transforming my pain into art and hope. In the depths of despair, I discovered the power of expression, and through my writing, I found a path toward healing.

As a gift, I offer you this collection I penned when I was 17 years old during my time at Clinton Correctional Facility. I discovered my voice, nurtured by the presence of my mother—even from afar. In a world that deemed us lost causes, she showed me potential where others saw despair.

What if she had been given the chance to flourish? What if the support systems had allowed her to thrive as a mother? I wonder how different our stories might have been, how my siblings and I might have known a mother fully present and cherished.

What I hold close is the beauty, wisdom, and nurturing spirit she embodied. Through her, I learned the vital lesson: love must be fed to those who need it most. What if grace were woven into the fabric of the child welfare system? How transformative that could be.

In the meantime, a poet emerged from the depths of my mother's love, teaching me that love transcends circumstances. It flows from mind to fingertips, finally meeting the world on the page.

Remember, *The Walls of a Gray Cloud* is a raw testament from the heart of my 17-year-old self. I invite you to immerse yourself in these pages, experiencing my words in their purest, most unfiltered form. Each poem is a glimpse into my soul—a vivid reflection of struggle and growth that I share with intention, allowing you to feel the weight, the horrors, and beauty of my journey. Misspellings and poor grammar notwithstanding,

If I could reach back through time, I would whisper to that young man: "Keep writing. Your voice has the power to uplift your mother and your family. Despite what others may say, know that your mother's love nurtured you, helping you to not only survive but to spread that love to others.

You are deserving. You are worthy. YOU are a poet."

Also, for you
My Brothers and Sisters
Wendy's Children
Nelly, Rebecca, Felipe, Pedro, Stephanie,
Michael, Gregory, and Samira

16 Poems

When I Was Three

When I was three,
They took me from her,
A sudden separation
from her tender embrace,
Her warmth—
a distant memory in the chill.

She never came
to soothe the searing pain,
From a blaze ignited within my young eyes,
My boyish heart could not fathom
Why did they bound her in churlish ways
Not to see me in her arms
but to see her in chains?

Shackled hands,
weary feet confined,
She vanished from my sight's embrace,
In the silence of her absence,
I grappled with a heart's cruel cage.

My mother, a shadow in my tender dreams,
I'll name her Mommy for this tale's sake—

For humanity's tender grace,
She herself was a beacon
I desperately sought.

In dreams,
I trace her soft and soothing lullabies,
Echoes of a time
before the system's cold grasp,
Her voice, a fleeting whisper in the winds,
A lull of love I long to clasp.

In crowded rooms, I search for her eyes,
A mirror of my own reflecting back,
Yet, the faces blur, and hope wavers,
A ghostly dance of vanished grace.
Years have passed like autumn leaves,
Each one a silent testament of her pain,
Yet the fire in my heart remains unquenched,
A flicker of the warmth I never gained.
I never gained
I never gained

Mommy's touch,

a memory unmade,
A timeless tale of separation's sting,
Her laughter lost to shadows' embrace,
An echo of what might have been.
Through countless nights,
the silence grows,
An empty space where her love once was,

I build my world on fragile dreams,
Seeking solace in the moon's soft pause.
Yet in the tapestry of time's embrace,
I craft my story,
piece by piece,
In the whisper of the wind,
I find her face,
A solace in a memory's sweet release.
And as I grow, I bear her name,
A tribute to a love both fierce and frail,
In every breath, I carry her flame,
Mommy,
forever in my heart's
eternal tale.

Moonlit FosterCare

They never let me look out a window…

The moon was on the other side
of the world,
and the door was closed
at the beginning.
I got a chair to reach the doorknob—
my thoughts traveled beyond,
wondering if my Mommy was there,
to bring me into her world
with a hug and kiss.

Night formed outside my window,
the stars disappeared.
Then my auntie barged into the room,
slipping her scaled, calloused hands
into my tinniness,

She said, "I'm sorry."
Saying nothing really,

She guided me through my first steps
on the sidewalk,

when the sky looked like a black hole
leading to another place.

We wandered through the hallways
of the project complex,
where I saw lilies and tulips
instead of red tops and broken glass.

She knocked on my grandpa's door,
and he sentenced me to my hell,
declaring he didn't want me—
to give me away to the police.

She obeyed him…
As she took my hand,
I felt myself falling,
the broken glass in the hallways
mirroring my own shattering.

Became broken glass
Shards of mirror mirroring wet cheeks
Like mosaic tears

"Where's my Mommy?"
She has a hug and kiss for me
that will chase away the scary things.

Cars with red, white,
and blue lights arrived,
echoing a cacophony of wired voices
as the doors opened

The sound invaded my little ears.
My eyes grew heavy,
my fingertips collapsed into my palms.
I could no longer reach out,
To touch my dreams anymore
my dreams slipped away
I now have a balled fist—

where is my mom?
Maybe she can do something.

And when this lady said she was in jail,
like the pigeons on the roof
who couldn't go anywhere,
because Tito said they can't,

the people in the car with the lights on them
are Mommy's Tito.

I was dragged into the car,
confusion wailing within me,
and I couldn't stop crying.
And the moon—the moon
the moon from the other side of the world—
suddenly appeared,
following me.

I noticed—
That the door,
that door
has a window.

Joselito's Blue

I didn't notice the sun rays
kissing the sharp edges of the fence,
Its glitter once magical
Every time I gazed out a window,
But the only windows allowed
were car-panes.

Trees and buildings danced behind me,
As my eyes traced their fleeting shapes,
I learned to think in abstractions,
A survival tactic against unseen chains.
Social workers grabbed me by the arms,
Pants suits pulled me to places
I knew weren't right,

My mother didn't return this time,
Her smile, a unique solace,
now out of sight.
Her touch had soothed me in ways
beyond others,
Nurturing me before my boyhood dawned,

As the sun's rays arrived,

painting skies with hues of me

I see sometimes in dreams
when my entire Mind opens wide
and I stare into possibilities,
possibilities that seem to be ending now

Darkness gave way to purples and reds,
Soft hues and a fondness for wrestling.
Yet, the blare
The blare of police radios
drowned the world's murmur,
I was being taken to my first foster home,

Unaware of the journey,
thinking of my mother,
Sadness streaked my cheeks,
my cries a muffled moan.

Amid sirens and choked sobs,
Someone called for my Mommy,
a fleeting hope,
Her arms, I long for,
To undo the knots in my chest,
a means to cope

her entire being
was always a means to cope
If only her fingers could caress my cheeks,
Seal her love with gentle kisses,
Everything would be alright,
I thought,
I still think
Yet I needed more than words,
a presence that glistens.
Her surety was a balm
only she could provide,

I lost her to the carceral veins
Carceral veins polluting my world,
At three years old, I lost my Mommy,
A loss too deep
for a young heart to have unraveled.

Now
in pieces…

Foster Boy on Rikers

And then…I became a foster boy
look what happened
My feet planted on a dream
Waking up from stings on my skin
Sometimes I am not there
disconnected from my body
As it gets pulled and torn in foster homes
Makeshift families
I don't belong to me it seems
I don't even belong to you it feels

Purple and blues…and red trails
on the canvass made of myself
Where I was hoping you'll kiss
Or hold
or press
Press through the soft beat of a pulse
and…and…and…

In reality.
They forgot my name.
They can't remember
the footprints of my tears,

the track marks of my fear.
When the gate closes
and the scream noises
are muffled by a corcrafted pillow,
And others yelling
through bars
On The Island
feeling close to a ghost,
On The Island
Close to a ghost
comforted with conditional hugs,
blood dripping
from the ceiling of cracks on the floor
where I walk the dirt becomes one
with life,

the struggle becomes curtained
Then…
The gate closes
And The scream noises
Are silenced and turned inward

How do I contain a scream
With my little lungs
When no one hears it,

the WORLD…ENDS

Now,
blind without braille to read,
lost without a compass,
gone without a casket.
ON The ISLAND!!
I'm feeling close to a ghost.

Out of sight, out of mind,
a fight in the dark Commences
not televised, not mentioned
to a soul.

I've been looking in this mirror
A fog for my reflection
I've been fighting with my image,
reaching to a portal,
freedom in the distance,
bang, bang,
screaming.
Screaming
and swinging
fighting demons

I was guilty as soon as I was born
With hints of cocaine in your veins

Now…Foster Boy on The Island
Close to a ghost
haunting your own shadow.
Your shadow chooses
to slither away from you

The SUN has vanished
each night may never end
You were 3 years old
when that night never ended
It's still going,

so at 16
Living in a dungeon
Was meant to be for me
Statistically I made it
A dream come true for the new BCW
Foster boy
feeling close to a ghost
now…
Each nap can be the last
like nothing no more.

Like there's no you no more

But…
But…
rather have demons kissing me goodnight
then kissing me Goodbye.

So I turn into them
riding through the nights with your pen,
drenching life with ink,
watering the seeds of knowledge with tears
Worms trickling down my cheeks,
Pressing onto my lips
through fingertips
on this Mothafucking pen

and this paper
between these lines I am binded
Binded with a seal of my thoughts
distilling arrested memories
I can only envision myself
With Leaves of grass
between Tiny Toes
Whitman taught me a lot
I read Keats

I read Ginsberg…
I've been howling inward
I read Gibran and traveled with Almustafa
Descending from the hill and weeping
before my heart flew open
Stretching my mind out

Yet Close to a ghost
balled up,
chin on my knees
crying outside,
dying inside
Bars muffling dreams.

Close to a ghost
As letters arrive
to haunt me in my reality.

They are yelling
As I guard my own casket
Taking ownership of things
that own me
Why?
Photos peppered on
the walls of what encases me

I die living
I die living
close to ghosts of the past

Out of sight,
still out of mind.

The needles of my past prick my mind
staring at memories
projected onto the ceiling.
Bandaging an engine,
bandaging wounds on my soul
with notebooks of poetry,
stories and songs Mommy gave me
close to a ghost.
Close to a ghost
Haunted
by a real-life person.

She Found Me There

Then…
She found me
Mommy…
You found me…
…finally…
She found me in a darkened corner,
Laced with resentment from her absence,
Loneliness,
a cloak of silent torment,
Yet Mommy sought me not,
but found her way.
Belonging was my yearning,
like August rays on a flower
these are the last moments of the summer

Warm rain on my skin,
seeping deep inside,
Where I buried seeds in shadows' retreat.
In the dark where I wished to hide.

I never knew I still longed for her embrace,
My Mommy's…Wendy's
Or that she was searching, ever near,

In a cell where rage and blood trace,
Her love's absence draws her here.
Within in me

She found me,
nudged me close through letters and verse,
In metaphors of love, our hearts immerse.
Each word a thread,
weaving freedom from chains,
A knitted garment of hope
where She needled with her fingers
And love remains.

Although we both lived in
In the margins of sorrow,
Child welfare said she wasn't equipped
to do what she was born to do
Love me

I resented her absence,
But now our dreams take flight,
Through letters and poetry
From C-74
Adolescents at war
To the Rosies facility

We gathered our strength,
My mother gathered her son

And…and…and

Whispers of strength arrived
in the stillness of my night.

That night that never ended,
Its still going…

Though shackles tethered us to each other,
they couldn't contain our longing
to leap and sever our song,
With every stanza written,
She proved them wrong.
Yeah Them…Them…Those social workers
who stood before a judge and said
"She's not fit"

I wonder
Who the fuck is you?
To say who doesn't belong to who?

In every line penned,

her spirit danced,
Her fierce love,
our unyielding allure
to cover each other with art…
art   art   art
echoes of us had always danced
where the thing with feathers perch
and the stained glass is see through

Ink spills like tears,
we transcend the cold of the steel
holding our bodies,
Her kisses in verses,
Her touch in every word.
When the page ended,
I rose from the dark,

My muse became my mom
Her soul intertwined,
igniting my potential—
Her kiss in ink
Her arms in grace.

'Till Ink Meets Paper

Handwritten notes to her firstborn son,
Love letters, tender and true
The only solace a prisoner clings to,
In a world where freedom's a distant view.
Photos and letters:
the lifelines of the confined,

The thing with feathers is in envelopes,
Words from the deepest corners of her soul,
Yet my Mommy couldn't share those parts with me.
With me...

All my life,
she was out of reach,
Her essence locked away, unspoken,
Until she found her first son
behind the same walls,
The same Rikers Island where
she had long been a prisoner.

At last,

at long last,
She could touch me,
Kiss me,
Hold me as only a mother can.
Not with her arms
but with her words
Love letters
In the harsh confines of Rikers Island,
New York City, the city that never sleeps,
A battleground of dreams and despair,
Her love battled against systemic trials
to keep her down.

Amidst the unyielding conditions,
We both lived as captives of fate,
Within walls where they hate us
They always hated us
Disguised as care was child welfare
Yet,
amid this cruel confinement,
My mother became the mom I needed.
Finally, her love letters and poetry
bridged the divide,
signing her letters
'Till Ink Meets Paper…Mommy

Rescuing me through the pen,
saving me from the abyss,

In our shared prison,
her presence transformed,
My mother became my salvation,
my true embrace
And then…
a Poet was born!

A Mother's Response
(My mom would write me poems like this
She loved this rhythmic pattern)

In the depths of my heart, a beacon shines,
Every reaching of yours is met with mine,
Though the walls kept us apart for years,
My love for you transcends trials and tears.

I see your face in the stars above,
In every tender memory, I hold your love,
The promise of touch,
the warmth of our bonds,
In every whispered hope,
you're the light that responds.

In the harsh world where shadows dwell,
I sent my heart through the cracks of hell,
Though my arms were restrained,
my spirit flew,
Reaching for you in every breath I drew.

Through the system's cold embrace,

my dear,
Know that my love was always near,

In foster care's darkness,
I dreamed of your smile,
Imagining our moments,
though separated by miles.

I yearned for the day when we'd reunite,
When the pain would end,
and love would ignite,
No apparatus could measure our true bond,
Your touch and my love
will forever respond.

Now, as we stand together, heart to heart,
Our story weaves a new, beautiful start,
In every embrace, every kiss, every sigh,
My love for you soars
beyond the sky.

I Remember Seeing You in Handcuffs

I remember seeing you in handcuffs,
walking into court,
The shiniest thing was your smile,
You were missing a tooth, quirky,
And I thought how funny, My Mommy.

I anticipated your hug,
my heart held tight,
Though the chains and cuffs
painted a stark scene,
The social worker let me see you,
In a world where our reunion
felt like a dream.
Fear of the unknown never haunted me,

Only absence loomed as the specter I dread,
The void of your presence
made my heart flee,
Trembling alone, my spirit misled.
Loneliness as a boy
felt like a miscarriage in community,

A loss too profound for words to unfold,
In a sea of faces, I felt a silent immunity,
Yearning for your touch, a hand to hold.

The courtrooms and their cold,
indifferent glances,
The clamor of justice,
a hollow refrain,
Yet amid all the harsh circumstances,
Your smile was a balm for my silent pain.
I waited through days, each hour a trial,
Your letters and love kept me from despair,
In every word, I found a fleeting smile,
A promise that soon,
I'd feel your care.
And now, as memories meld with the
present day,

I see how you struggled,
your enduring fight,
In every hardship,
in each gentle sway,
You wished I knew
Your love had been my guiding light.

Our reunion, a tapestry of scars and grace,
Woven through the trials
we've both endured,

In the spaces between a sacred place
And me
Where love and resilience
Have never been secured.

I remember seeing you in handcuffs
Maybe that's why I wore them too

Her Name Across My Eyes

Her name etches itself upon my vision,
Each time I glimpse the depth of her gift—
Words on paper,
tender echoes from the past,
Arriving when my heart was most in need.

Handwritten notes
that spoke of love's embrace,
Yet too late for kisses I had longed for,
Since I was three, yearning in the dark,
Now sixteen, bound by chains of longing.
In shackles worn by her through the years,
A mirror of my own confined state,
Moments missed where
her presence was missed,
I find myself still craving her tender grace.
When a boy is lost,
consumed by stormy thoughts,
Haunted by shadows of worthlessness
Only one voice can chase away the lies,
Or Mommy's kiss,
her touch, her loving care.
What happens when

her presence is sealed away,
Locked in a chest of memories unclaimed?
Mommy's essence, once a guiding light,
Now a ghost in a cage of enduring pain.

Yet in dreams and whispers,
her warmth persists,
A comfort in the silence of her absence,
Her love remains,
a gleaming through the night,
Mommy's ways,
a solace amidst my plight.

In every trial, her spirit guides my path,
Even as I wear the chains she once bore,
Her strength and grace shaped my journey
In the echoes of her words
and whispered vows,
I found my way through darkness.
Because of her

Tears for Wendy

Why this reaching if not for you
Where the first thing to love
Was your face
with the promise from your touch
From the galaxies you see in me
To the joy in your arms

Of course this is a reaching for you
When the first thing I felt
Felt so good to try more
And without ABCs or 123s
I can figure out forever

So why this reaching for you
When the system has bleeding arms
They Carried me with
Held me with their stares
before the stairways
Where mommy's and daddy's
perverse the title

All the resources are there
to fail in foster care

And nothing to reflect your touch
No apparatus to look you in your eyes
And see cuddles and laughter dance
On the floor between your skin and
What holds you up
A voice for a doorbell and
eyes for letting in the sun
So why this reaching for you, Mommy?

My Muse,
Because I love
that I remember

Colorful Shards of Mirror

My mirror shatters, falling
Into vibrant, fractured pools,
Becoming scattered shards
That reflects fragmented parts of me.

Her fingertips slipped away,
Lost to gang culture's dark grasp,
Cupid's arrows turned to concrete tips,
Foggy mirrors in the agency's cold embrace,
Where the devil wears the mask of systems.
They look at me,
Seeing a boy trapped in chains,
A state-sanctioned assault
on my very being,
Reduced to pieces, scattered and raw.

The child welfare system,
The 'They' I speak of
see me as a product,
A mere cog in their cruel machine,
I refuse to be defined by their harsh gaze,
Their stripping away,
their dehumanizing hands.

In their attempt to rebuild me with iron,
I remain in fragments,
Shards of mirror, colorful and true,
Reflecting my own complex identity.

Yet, amidst the chaos,
An entire government
Suppressing her ability to be a Mom
Cloaking behind a dark veil
for me not to see
Her desire to touch me
with her nurturing presence

she reached me with poetry
and love,
Delicate and precise,
To piece me back together with tender care,

My Mommy's loving touch
reformed the shattered glass.
And then…a poet emerged,
Born from the fragments,
To face the world anew,
Guided by the love that mended the pieces.
To get back in touch with her

A Mother's Song

My dearest child, in trials deep and dark,
I've found you through the storm,
a guiding light,
In every letter sent, a tender mark,
A beacon shining in your endless night.
Though distance and despair
have held you tight,
My love has soared
through prison's heavy bars,
With every verse,
I've tried to ease your plight,
And heal your wounds
beneath the prison's stars.
My heart beats with the rhythm
of your pain,
I've reached you
through every written word I send,
And though the system tried to
break the chain,
Our bond remains,
unyielding,
without end.

As soon as letters clear the guarded gate,
I'll hold you close,
my love, it's not too late

Her Arms: My Song

In the stillness of dawn, they came for me,
With cold hands and stares like sharp steel,
I clung to her, my world crumbling silently.
Her arms, once a fortress, felt the strain,
As I was pried away, my tears fell like rain,
In that fleeting moment, I felt only pain.

The walls seemed to close,
the air grew thin,
Her whispers were lost in the clamor within,
Each step away felt
like a wound to my skin.
The car door slammed, sealing our divide,
Her anguished face, a silhouette outside,
In the rearview, her sorrow was a tide.
In the foster home's sterile, silent halls,
I wondered if her heart still felt my calls,
How do you mend a young heart that falls?
Yet amidst this loss,
do you see your strength,
In the shadows of despair,
can you find your strength?

Will you rise from the ashes,
reclaim your day,
And turn your pain into a beacon's ray?

Wish My Love Was The Vaccine (Bilingual Version)

I've been crawling through this life
Motherless
Deprived from flying through the sky
'cause my wings were clipped
Sin madre
Privado de volar por el cielo
porque mis alas fueron cortadas

My strength was toddler
I was just 3 when I was banned
from the pursuit of happiness
Celebrate myself
when I was deprived from family

I had no power
I had no voice
no tenía poder
No tenía voz
I was motherless
Motherless

And she was alive breathing

Crawling through the mud
to disguise her beauty
Y ella estaba viva,
Arrastrándose por el barro
para disfrazar su belleza
On a journey not chosen for her really
Sniffing through a straw to hide her reality
Blanketed by the black ice
that covered her journey
She wasted her kisses
Ella desperdició sus besos.
on conditional love
when I yearned for her hug

And I was blind
estaba ciego
Estaba asustado por una hoja que no podía
ver llamada cocaína
I was scared by a blade
I couldn't see called cocaine
I didn't know that monster's name
that kidnapped her
Leaving me motherless
Motherless
Mami

And she was alive breathing
My father was engaged in the pipeline
Papi
A rolling stone
styling his methods on 2 sides
2 sides of the journey
dos lados del viaje
One of them my mother
Mami
The other
The virus that causes AIDS
SIDA
That virus that stole
my mother's golden hue

Now on a journey as a foster boy
I peeked through every peep hole in the sky
Miré por cada mirilla en el cielo.
And saw pissy hallways in the clouds
next to my dreams
Floors covered with crack vials
Vidrios rotos, visiones destrozadas
esparcidas por las calles
Broken glass,

shattered visions peppered on the streets
And screams by the crowd
That's muffled by the darkness
As my fathers venom spit
Sucked up by my mothers straw
He gave it to her

se lo dio a ella.

On a journey
Where my mom could have been yours
Mi mama puede ser la tuya
Now, on a journey
Wish my love was the vaccine
Ojalá que mi amor fuera la vacuna.
Wish my love was the vaccine for HIV

And she died dreaming,
alive breathing
now she is through me
Y ella murió soñando,
respirando viva a través de mí.
And as she captures back her crown from
leaving me down
I understand the journey

She was on the ground
Reaching for a hand
Reaching for her man
He gave her pain
Left her on the dirt
With her skirt next to the flame
Él le dio dolor
La dejó en el suelo
Con su falda junto a el infierno
That burned for 20 years
20 years
20 years filled with tears
Fears filled with cries
Felt like I died
When she asked me to forgive her
My mother
Wrapped on a journey of turmoil
Asked me to forgive her
Oh. Mommy
mami
Oh Mommy
I wish
I wish my love was the vaccine
for all things ugly

Ojalá que mi amor fuera la vacuna para
todas las cosas feas
Para que podamos celebrarnos
a nosotros mismos.
So that we can celebrate ourselves
On journey of peace
To be the thing
We all need to be
Ojalá que mi amor fuera la vacuna
para sanar todas las cosas.

Wish my love was the vaccine
to heal all things
Mami
Oh mami
Wish my love was the vaccine
Wish my love was the vaccine
Wish my love was the vaccine for all things

The POETS of ME b/c of MOMMY

I can only envision myself
Almustafa answers the townsmen
Ginsberg sets off a Howl
and I'm down in blue hues

Trying to perch with
Leaves of grass
between Tiny Toes

I exploded in poetry
Raised up by men who were in chains
Saw the little boy inside a yard full of men
Reciting pain

I intended to love on myself
like They never did before
I now have a muse to live up too
My mommy

My Mommy
Instilled within me a survival tactic

Who do I turn to if not myself

when the hollowest of beings live next door
Yet these human souls gathered me
Sheltered me in my lessons
Allah's mathematics
the geometry of hope.

As I needed something
to reflect into the world
How do I express this expressive soul!
Locked away for the next 20 years
with dreams aching to break free?

What do I do?
I write

I write poetry to hold me down
crafting verses that rise like wind to flames,
each line a step toward freedom,
my golden crown forged in ink and heart.
I can only envision myself,

With every stanza,
I learn to stand tall,
to honor the art that shapes me,

and to embrace the encouragement
from those who raised me
Those who have walked
Through hardened journeys,
men who once wore gang colors
now tasked with raising a boy into a man,
each poem a testament to our path,
each word a brushstroke of resilience
An Exodus at Exodus
on the canvas of my life
They poured into me
And I poured out

I poured out
MY SOUL

Almustafa answers the townsmen,
Ginsberg unleashes a howl,
and here I am, drenched in blue hues,
trying to perch with the thing with feathers
Leaves of Grass between my toes
My tiny toes.
I explode in poetry,

Now, I have a muse to live up to—
My Mommy,

My Mother

So yes,
I witnessed my mother
Taken away from me
At 3 years old
So taking anything away from me?
Had become a normal thing.

Disguised to me was something
That grew into resentment
Something that was made to burn
The system
The system
was
Made to burn
the roots of her
But

I witnessed my mother
Taken into me
Disguised to me
was something
That grew into resentment
Something that was made to burn

Made to burn the roots of her

Her voice, once a lullaby,
Turned into echoes of pain
Searing leaves glowing into smoke
Budding into the next home
like wildfires do

But I have Memories of her laughter
flickering
Fading into crackles
distant cries,
Yet her spirit lingered,
As my ghost of love.

In the darkness of our separation,
I clung to the fragments of her smile.

A mother and son
both locked inside cages
yet
Her poems whispered solace,
And in the silence,
I heard the promise
of a brighter dawn

Our Letters became our lifeline,
Each word a bridge to hope,
Binding our broken hearts with ink.
Through steel bars
and cold nights,
We shared a hidden strength,
A resilience born of love and loss.
In her absence,
I found the courage to face my fears.
Dreams of freedom danced in my mind,
In A world where we could heal together.

Then…the guards came to remind me
that her body was not her own,
a vessel adrift in a sea of confinement.
The letters I cherished,
The thing with feathers soft and delicate,
were seized from by people
Wearing uniforms for horns,
They came again
To try take everything from me again

Blue looks ugly sometimes
Hoof prints on cell floors
secreting poison

But not from their feet
From the entire system
My spirit was plucked bare
before they casted her letters
into another dungeon's shadows.
They attacked our wings
just as we begun to soar,
perched on the ledges of light blue lines,
where ink flowed like blood,
pumping life into
the hollow spaces of my soul.

But they took it all—
stripped me bare,
then stole every single leaf of my dreams,
the pages that had served as our wings,
a sanctuary where words danced like
fireflies in the dark.

Mommy,
Though I no longer hold
your written words,
You carry within me
the tapestry of your love,
woven into the very fabric of my being.

With every breath and heartbeat,
I offer you this: Poetry—from my body

But poetry that came from you
And they said you were unfit
Yet They gave me
the language of my resilience,
a flight path traced in whispers,
where every line is a tribute,
a testament to the unbreakable bond
that even the thickest bars cannot sever.
Her love letters
calmed the storm in my eyes
The looming potential
That my growth will never realize
its brighter shine

To embrace the world in love
Makes you think different

Her pieces of reflection
from the shattered mirror
Shards picked up
by the twirling wind of my softness
I knew I had a softness

I tried to tell everyone
wow…
I wonder…
I can wonder now…

who taught you how to dream?
And…
…How often do you get a chance
to put a heart back together?

'Till Ink Meets Paper, Love your Son"

Presenting
(In its raw form, grammatical errors included)

The Walls of A Gray Cloud
(in Fragments)
By 17 year-old Me

A foster care child, now a prisoner with no idea that he will be free one Day!
Clinton Correctional Facility
Feb 2003-Feb 2004

RAMPAGE

"And the tongue is a fire, a world of iniquity:
so is the tongue among our members, that if defileth the
whole body and setteth on fire the course of nature; and it
set on fire of hell."

- JAMES 3:6

RAMPAGE

by: JOSE PEREZ

I dwell in the light that guides my path
through raft of life I get the math
that I could ride on the edge and get there last
grab my neck and chock it fast
ancient words by cash
fate that knows the last
breath you breathing gas
Fuck!, The screams go past
you don't hear me
got to be tough so they won't see bluff
plus!, they don't see me

I dwell in the dark and hope to glow
let them know this bomb about to blow
mouth foams when your thoughts is getting cold
so I got to aim the tongue and flow
pain is good to know
words were meant to fold
tricks is getting old
blood in need for coal
you don't get it
got to be hurt so this pen could work
Man!, you don't get it

RAMPAGE (P.2)

got to sleep first
so these dreams could alert you from losing it

I dwell in a mind that hopes for war
still I know my guts is wanting more
so I add fuel to words and call it raw
and I know what your eyes is waiting for
I'm going to guide this tour
Fuck the Fucking law!
pass but don't touch my door
God is short for Lord
So I'll make it
Plant my feet well
so these steps could tell
if I'll make it
17 shells going to put me through hell
but I'll make it!

PIPE LINE

by: JOSE PEREZ

Death is a privilege
pain is cause you punished
a repercussion
you just got love
I thought of
the facts
         tator
the rush
and later
the truth going to flourish
I ain't going to say
some people start praying and
on the low
the organism don't know when
the pain comes
it hurts
brain thinking of death
not even a small amount of mass
from an atom is left
train of thought dead
flik the fucking lead
he under the shed
he can't sleep as he

PIPE LINE (P.2)

lays in his bed
idea's roam deep
when he is shedding his red
and who said
he wants to be tortured
he wants to do it
so when you hear about it
you say that
he never ran
he always had it
he grabbed it
he never lost because he always was boss
it was a cost he had to pay
you know what they say
a check he couldn't cash
his life ended so fast
they made his throat gag
from the tip of a mag
but then
at last
bullet to his dome
stopped him
Lucifer already been shown
he's on his own
IN HELL!

DEEP DOWN

by: JOSE PEREZ

Coming into then out of the darkness of your womb
my frail mind with out a clue
of what this hell would bring
I don't know what was the first thing I saw
but I hope it was the middle of the room
The bulb that defines truth
come to think about it
I was your first born male
so why was I left alone to guide my own at 4
it comes to dawn that you weren't ready for me
so why give me a name?
why name me?
it was in your power
but you did not deserve to give me my attribute
so I renamed
I-Build Powerful Reality Allah.
It wasn't you who defined and confined to my life
It was me
you chose that
I dreamed of a fictitious life in heaven with you
by my side and him
but that did not comply
for it couldn't apply to what was planned
for me

DEEP DOWN (P.2)

BARS.

Now that, wasn't your fault

but you vanished after

31,536,000 seconds

or 35,040 hours

or 1,460 days to be exact

but in your terms it was only 4 years

dam, why mom?

But fuck that

that I deserve

I incriminated my self into the street life

learned on my own

I'm hurt

I can't write no more.

LET ME REST

by: JOSE PEREZ

Give me room
my eyes sparked the boom
the clocks stopped my doom
the breeze shook the bloom
give a fuck about a wound
I'm the blood in my scars
I'm the light in those stars
I'm the steel in these bars

It's hard when a little boy's mind close
but he's far
got a stranger pulling his cards
while he got his heart guard
but it's not hard
to get used to the pain
'cause who's to blame
when those clouds can't rain
errands bring a stain to your brain
and in a chain
you ain't feeling the same
your heart is insane

WHY?, is the question

- LET ME REST

the sky is your destination
watch me lie in my station
pop the color of your eyes
they red,
and mothafuckaz don't give a fuck
if I lay in a bed at 17.
with out a dream
in your head there's a beam
that carries a bullet that nobody seen
It's sweet dreams to darkness
my sheet and my blanket
I'm ready to cop it

let me rest my god-body
let me rest my pump-shoty
they claim I'm nobody
I am supreme being
let me cool down my life's steaming
I see the skies gleaming
I'm ready to meet my sun
to watch my soul leaving
let me rest please
let me get the point of this
boil my fist
shatter the mirror that keeps telling me shit

LET ME REST

the clock think he wise
cause he telling me the time
but I don't need numbers to know the math
the blast from an atom controls the mass
they really don't know
were my stash at
tell me were you from
how you walk
I'll prove your ass cat
this metal part of my heart
got me jumping out the box
I seize spots
while it hurts to see organism die
paint a picture, why?
I doubt my soul flies to the sky
that I need to survive
to strive for the whole pie
but most guys bitch
no lie, real bitch
they curl up
hold there face moaning
a man ain't supposed to die owing
they supposed to die growing
but before I start building
let me rest my god-body.

IT'S MY TURN

by: JOSE PEREZ

The crack of my bones pierces my ears
with cold drooling visions
IT'S MY TURN
A time when vengeance screams with joy
A time were my intentions would not be avoid
I'm tired
I'm so tired
no one will detect the mask no more
and I'm real sure
that no walking 2 legged organism
will delete my presence
from the photographic part of there minds
its not possible
IT'S MY TURN

A gloomy shadow follows my instinct
understand my purpose
They tried
they so tried

I'm alive breathing
the fact that you slipped
your eyes were narrow
and burnt a hole in my heart

IT'S MY TURN   (P.3)

that grind and tried to backlash at my existence
They failed because I'm here
Between these walls and these bars and me
I'm here
leery towards anything that could happen
knowing that situations are unlimited

But the remembrance of were it all started
is locked in my conscious to encourage my vision
And it appears to you different?
It appears to you unfair?
Well, me too

My own shadow
My own people threw in the towel
because of my existence
An infant
Practically an infant
You betrayed your obligation of loyalty
I hurt every day
But you know what?
I cry a river explaining this, but,
IT'S MY TURN BITCH, IT'S MY TURN.

IT'S MY TURN   (P.2)

you hurt me
Glorifying the day when you will one day
be different
That dream was crushed
before my mind could race to another thought
It tortured my infant great mind
IT'S MY TURN

These words erupt like an irritated
Hawaiian mountain
my pulse races with abnormal beats to my flesh
I feel it
and as i pull my hair
I question
I answer
I quiver with anger
I observe the future with out a doubt in my mind
I control my premeditating conscious
Its over
IT'S MY TURN
IT'S MY GO
Her too, I remember
I remember the clouds convulsing its content
It reminds me of every storm that struck
the hollow in the sky

MASK

by: JOSE PEREZ

A lesson was made to be given to star
in a mist of a pitch black world
No knowledge or understanding to why
thought that I will stay standing
and take these walls ramming and be left to die.

I had another plan
an action verb to the opposite of stand
and take everything that revealed it self
to the knowledge of my eyes.

I became worked out
forgot my purpose and got knocked out by this wind
reformed from observing and coping with in
mentally naked
moved to dodge light and be labeled a so-called
but most of all
I played with energy that was great
with controlling and deceiving ways
in swimming through fate

Escaped bared fruit
symbolized as understanding to why
I asked why?

MASK (P.2)

When the wind wiped the virgin
and exposed my main organ
natures orphan
I'm disguise when I'm living a lie
so in reality I'm skipping through lines
Not remaining conscious of the realness
of the foundation of the bomb
Why the boy is long gone
now a man sits on a curve
watching his palms gripping some steel
suddenly all around me is still
and the will of my being is cold
but this is why the Scriptures of mind
was formed in a fold
so you could see the actual feeling
that I really should be
But I could control were a man should walk
through the black stone
cracking the side of my dome
shivering the root of my bones
and I remain alone in this hell
against all beings that couldn't tell
I'm taking it off
My eyes red cause I'm pissed off
I'm hurt

IT'S REAL LIKE THAT

by: JOSE PEREZ

The sound screams in my ear
waking me up out of a dream I wish was real
"walking on 12"
just to see if every bodies here
but every bodies here
"Yo!, Put out the bones"

Invisible puddles are forming in beds
and some bodies stay here
is written in stone forever
MAX DATE: 9999
clenched fist don't matter
but a clenched eye-lid
is a feeling of pain
and a whole lot of weight
I CRY
every time I look at such date

He feels real alone when his neighbor
receives some words from the bird
some people are more fortunate than others
He don't give a fuck though (yeah right!)

Top Cat grilling his face

IT'S REAL LIKE THAT (P.2)

waiting to put a cork in it
some shit he did in the county
I do the knowledge
he gone in a week

Territorial minds don't hold back
cause whatever piece of shit you had
turns sacred
they will guard it
but then one day
you going to have to put his face through it
whatever it is
Now dig'um up
Because his mans
didn't like that
Lets start this scrap
IT'S REAL LIKE THAT
dam!
shit is real.

NEED NO ONE

by: JOSE PEREZ

I posses a vision that
I surely make it through hell
I made a decision that either stay pist in
all I become is a man that stays faking
with the false characterization
that I have to stay
what I need to do is find the last rule
and break through
these bars of heaven in hell
fuck the story to tell
cause all a leader did was lead to a cell
now he claiming fuck that
Cause I think he can't take it
when the needle pierces the pain
the real reason why the cloud
just hits him with rain
out of the mist of a lame
I got to calm down

I posses a vision
that I'll surely make it through hell
work for my mind to prevail
inner-city in the core of my brain

NEED NO ONE (P.2)

so the diagnosis could consider me well
But only I could
how the fuck could he tell
I done did it
It done happened
A decision that made an action
but they ain't really feeling me
I got to brain storm and build in me
My eyes rolling in the back of my head
But the pain ain't killing me

Give me more
fuck two
give me four
show me it's war
nothing could stop my third eye
when its formulating a plot
as I walk my head got my hands gripping a boulder
get the fuck off me
I get out of the mist of hell
dusting dirt of my shoulders

REMEMBER THE PAIN
by: JOSE PEREZ

Rapidly given a glance
to a picture that triggered
the memory of hell
such pain denies me cure
the plants keeps growing
it hurts

My tears blow away
to calm down the nerves that stay
pressing my hands
while it shakes violently
concentrating to stop
but failed cause my heart never forgot
the tribulation that I went through
All of its pain never forgotten
and impossible to be forgiven

I'm like a fly stuck in a web
struggling to get out and made it
remember the set of eyes
of the 8 legged mutant
that was licking his lips staring at me
Never again will I go through such thing

REMEMBER THE PAIN   (P.2).

I am going to treat my understanding like prince

The abuse will   man insane
with a black
ready to take   that crowned him
whether it was   good
he didn't care
you know what it was that claimed him king?
cause now he serves a life to survive in a cage

The power of equality
reigns supreme
cause Allah sees equality in Peace!
But I remember the face that created a monster
to be more specific
I remember the face
I remember the pain given to me
by my father

PAIN

by: JOSE PEREZ

It hurts when sad literature pulls the trigger
then you sit there and wonder
why placement was done
coming amongst your emotions it hurts so bad that
you refuse to use metaphor and you asked to that:
What for?, I mean,
how could the circumference of your environment
be so painful to the young?
bouncing off from place to place
A mind to waste
wondering when will fate play its role
Ol'Earth trapped in bars missing the stars,
plus the sun vanished
as that star grows into it's atomic self
it manifest something to happen, something to happen
A mind lacks fine facts contacts to his world
in aspects of everything that's less
feeling's is not worthy
down the drain is the main membrane that hurts
I can't talk, I can't scream,
I can't determine what seems
Because I want a particular place in the universe
But when the vein on my neck bursts, It hurts!

THE MAKING OF A BOMB
by: JOSE PEREZ

Explosion
leaning towards the floor
dining in the streets
time keeps ticking
a person that is less
plus stress
keeps building
moms ain't there
strangers is always there
can't see the good
what a confused person
its sad
scheming
studying
striking
give me give me give me
right hands pointer finger and thumb
keeps going in my mouth
elevation
it doesn't work
opportunities to unity
distractions that you let
the papers
a reminder

THE MAKING OF A BOMB (P.2)

Tears turn into rage
fuming looking all around
disgusted
cursing, still no bursting
hurting
stumbling
reaching, no one is there
screaming
tightening
a feeling so frightening
you don't even know
still you haven't blown
a hair ball in your heart
don't look at me, don't talk to me, don't touch me
never knew there will one day be a time
when I can't set that line
rules? there are none
and there's a whole ton
fuck them jibber jabber power head mothafuckaz
fuck you
but hold me
Dam!, Nah!, fuck that don't touch me
I stiffen
explosion
I'm dead.

I AM MY OWN FATHER

by: JOSE PEREZ

I woke up one day at 43 years old
wondering why moms soul so cold
neglect was so around my realm
sadness turned into angry thoughts
angry thoughts turned into uncontrollable emotions
I showed me how to ride a bike
I showed me how to read and write
I gave me a hand when there wasn't no light
I was me's mentor
I played catch with me
I went fishing,
nah!, I'm lying
I didn't go fishing
I remained wishing
I survived all the trials and tribulations
I went from crawling to walking to talking
now I stoop down to pacing in silence
Me was the referee that put my hand up
It was me not you
you fucking low life
but thank you
I'm the man that you failed
to mark your presence in my heart to teach him

I AM MY OWN FATHER (P.2)

The worlds got to pay for no days
but they congratulate me with a happy fathers day
but I need more than that

I cried on my own shoulder
I hyped my self up to get bolder
I lied for me
I survived with no lead
I protected my skin with my own mind
I was the antidote and the mixture
of a mother and father
I prepared my own test
I was my own pest
my own problem
My own prisoner for 15 years
blood and tears
and dears to a so-called god
asking why but never got an answer
I deserve an answer but I don't get it
children in Africa need cures but they don't get it
so why I be set aside as different
let alone I rot in prison
I was my own father but not a good one
Hey! I tried
did pretty well for Brown guy

I AM MY OWN FATHER (P.3)

That was down and dirty
and hands with rope burns and knees all swollen
they stay like that for a reason
It just gets worse and inside my head
I can't even imagine how much injuries it has
but to fall down completely
would be a thought that's last in choice
because every night I hear one voice
Keep going stupid
don't stop now
I didn't tie you down you clown
so keep searching for the day
you could catch wreck on deck
were every bodies watching
and understanding
don't get vex
earn your respect
to let go
man don't bother
after all those roads
you are your father.

STRAIGHT HELL

by: JOSE PEREZ

Why I wipe my tears before they fall?
they have no power
can't put out the flames
that boils my insides and my brain cells
and its just those slight burns that hurt the most
the spot were it does?
my heart
roam through so many lands
so many mine fields
that intend to soul-control my soul
my soft but so bold soul

My arms race for touch to prove
that I am close to change
but I made more than one glance to that path
but its like I will run forever
just to reach good weather

Please is what I beg for
begging for a chance
but dam!,
pain before fate
so early its late

STRAIGHT HELL   (P.2).

and late is never
straight hell
that's my story and have to stick to it
because if I don't
I'll probably go through it again
even though I'm still in it
I know
Cold steel is sharp
not a gun but cold steel is dark
long nights hands ready to rip my skin off
knuckles all swollen
plus you keep looking at that rope
veins bursting eyes closing neck burning
another topic for a C.O.

Straight fucking hell
I can't believe that hell keeps following me
I leave black foot prints behind me
why do I see strangers on my walls
no incoming calls
you feel like what you have
nothing at all
nothing at all
then the bell rings
and Ms. Rubenstein reminds me this is hell.

I'M STILL THINKING
by: JOSE PEREZ

Experience a place were you could sing freely
glide with the waves of the air
experienced minds just watch as you suffer
from that cool breeze
you become an experiment to man-kind
and you can't stop thinking your glad
because you get switched on and off
and they pick a stage everyday
the stages are different everyday
people do not know or understand
the rhythm of my thoughts
the way the float is its real strange
look deep down in this word
and see if it lives or exist
see if pain lashes out at my wrist
or see if love kisses my lips
I question why I asked to the question I asked
because you really don't know
the answer to the question they asked
but these nerves bop up and down
to a chorus of music
irritating the vein on my neck
bothering me to a song of death

but at the same time I'm blessed
I take my left hand and wipe my left eye
as I write on blood marked stained paper
because I gave it my all
I'm obligated to bum rush life with
3 hands and a pen
but I exist now to live, When?
people black and blue my veins
that pump words through my mind
just to see if my brain could take pain
they found out that my brain
could take more than that
my third eye could give and take amounts
like a mother with her dead seed
or a foster child back to the same scene
I bleed tears which means I cry blood
it hurts like a slipped hammer to a finger
it burns my chest and boils my throat
it fills my lungs up with dust bunnies
so I cough up words and thoughts
the pain feels good though
let me tell you this though
I know people tend to get confused
about the expressions and feelings I shed
but I am soft

I'M STILL THINKING (P.3)

not because I'm scared
because I lie and cheat
and fake sorrows and weep
I'm soft because I love to be fake
so for my sake I'll lie today
you don't have to understand my life
just look at this pattern of a so-called good life
they say god gave his best to take care of my being
but you know what?
fuck what he is seeing
because I am leaving this torture
I'm tired
I'm already in a grave of gray rocks
and platinum locks
and iron doors that cover me
I'm already in caged grass
and locked down birds that sing at night
I'm already in zeroes in ones that tell you my rights
I'm already covered in a room
with stopped toilets and black sinks
I'm already in a mirror of cement
that reflects dirt to my eyes
but for now I can't wait for a night to be mine
when I could hold the moon and my hands
and feed light to my flesh and bones

I'M STILL THINKING (P.4)

```
        track  keeps  trains  running
but             finish
                fill  up  my  head  with  car  oil
so   I       keep  going
        these  creatures  think  I'm  mad
            pist
    in  this  set  of  groups
       lashes  out  to  whats  really  wrong
```
the wrong behind the wrong
but its crazy
because I always tend to come back
to the back panel of whats not really real
I seek a life
a life to be free
a life were I don't have to worry about
doing good or doing bad
I could just sit back and drink sweet and light coffee
reminisce into the moments
were I could just flash my life in front of me
love the pastures that flow beneath
serene in a place of gold
but my heart fails!
my heart denies serene
and shoots blood up my eyes
that pop the color of my pupils

I'M STILL THINKING (P.5)

    its crazy because I take it
like 10 rounds to a vest
 lus I love the stress
whatever happens I leave it
  er change
       in pen so the pen won't erase
      the pain would be like taking my life
  ing my heart
  ing my spine
and then breaking my legs
so I let the pen flow
cause there time to take and there's time to let go
let this pen flow and go
in other words,
I need pain like water
I wouldn't shed a tear
I wouldn't punch a wall
I wouldn't dive in a curve to let go
a pillow to engrave my face in
I love it
I want to be tortured
don't change your mind
because you think I'm done
I never ran!
I stood there with my flesh in my hands

I'M STILL THINKING (P.6)

urple and black
bleeding in ice
hat cooled my experiences
I stood right there
     upon a peak
were you saw me and you didn't do shit
    probably laughed
    he bracelets lashed out at my wrist
    so mad
they some things happen for a reason
whats the reason for 15 years in a ditch of pain?
whats the reason?
I ask my self
not you
because you really not here
they just put that in my head
and it brain washed a lot of people
but me? not here!
I wish were a night could end
when I could see day light with a naked eye
I see my path but I wish to talk and walk
through it
I see a way to go through
but I just can't move
I see a rope to grab

I'M STILL THINKING (P.7)

    ut

    I hjust can't reach it
      pain I love it .
t for me to suffer I knew it
'll go through it
    ll seek to perfect this storm
but you know what?
    ll seek to connect my path
    perfect the wrong
  ': strength?
I remain strong
my mind is held up
and I cry a river
this life slithers through winners
and still tends to lose
I need a boost
but this pain moves this pen
with fingers that lets the ink
run smoothly through this faucet
of hurt, lust and love
I place my hand on my thigh
my right hand on my knee
I look up at the sky
and question who I be
and I'm still thinking
and I was thinking

120

I'M STILL THINKING   (P.8)

but today
  t yesterday not tomorrow
    now right here
  u see me
    you see me with a curious vision
that makes an assumption
    in all reality all you see me is as,

    you see me as is a weak man in prison
but I'm here to tell you
that just because your pictures perfect
and your path is clean
and your life is well outside
and your brain distills quotables
from the King James or Qu'ran
but you think your game
doesn't concern that pawn
your wrong
whats going on deep in the flesh
deep in your temple
because the stones on your wall
and the designer glass on your door
might be beautiful
that might not be refutable I must insist
but when that 5 minute situation or confrontation

121

`I'M STILL THINKING   (P.9)

or experience triggers that flash back
    in your peace
  r knowledge
    so-called peace
    ;
      ny your hurting inside
    use I could see the gold around you
        could see the multi-stained steel in you
      that out
  le ve it out
  be born
  now I'm just thinking

LEARY

by: JOSE PEREZ

  iet in the distance
     ach quick because I'm dying
       ed in this quilt of sorrow
h   rsona
lov y birds singing to my pace
     s second whirled world
s d life-time in the same time-span
    ing with the wind just because I can
I bang on any stand off
that makes me nervous
I approach with cushioned bullets
I love. I love.
I love the fierce touch of an angel
shadows upon my roof
do not give you permission to label
whether I'm normal ˀr stable
I black out negative electrons
I'm hesitant to step on
a heated up gangsta with a mask on

CHAOS

by: JOSE PEREZ

    p me in a corner, Scream!
    trical shocks through your breath
p   al voices, uncomfortable embraces
with bribes of death
    ions with fierce winds
      blow the curtains off of windows
so strong they blew my candles out
it dark.
there's a heaven that's false
there's a heaven that's truth
there's mouths that just talk
but there's false love that groom on ignorance.
It's sick.
hammer the nail in its place
uncensored words that pierce your heart with cold
Ice burning, frostbite truth
I make mine ruthless
cause it seems like iron don't hurt
like nouns don't work to boost and jerk your mind ba
bring back nature
bring back who you really are
plus you switch your self on
then you off that same spo
pace through a dead mind
observe and respect it enough to give it back it's s
and make one born the rest.

REASONS, ROSES, GASES & STEEL
by: JOSE PEREZ

Th smell of rusted steel penetrates my senses harshly in a world of ugliness. Confused with scriptures written by 's before me. Comparing them to modern day reality with in me. Burning in a dream would wake up any man or woman but did consciousness put out those flames? I guess it didn't. Because I still smell the stentch of flames burning upon human flesh. I guess this world has buried itself in anger so powerful, dreadful, malicious and so eager to let it's twin know who she is and why it must die in the past and be awakened by noise of guilt. Be awakened to over comp green leaves, purple roses and show the darkness in it's soil. Turmoil must defeat divine cell structures to up hold it's name.

It's strange how she goes up and down, down and up, side to side to make sure high explosives are served upon everyone who transgressed against the laws of Supreme chronological order. It's more of a celebration of war. Baring some power. Just enough to kill those lilies that are stuck in an illusion, to teach those who are content with lies in there dreams.

Understanding is difficult to be understood when a white sheet covers all eyes that tend to think they see when they are blind. They rewind to the time when there backs was faced to the graffiti and blood splattered in there faces and there tennis shoes. So cruel intentions are made before one has a thought, they are aware of.

REASONS, ROSES, GASES & STEEL   (P.2)

They strike with strength that is foreign to their own knowledge. There own village is destroyed by the hands that created the spark to even build it in the first place. Not a trace is left for future souls to feed there hungry eyes with light. They leave after self destruction and roam with heavy suitcases of different colors and moods and things no one understands so they label it stupidity, they label it crazy, mentally insane. They only came up front and personal with the outcome. To the life that the past made with beedy eyes, bloody drool, purple and black nails that drenched the minds city with vengeance. Retaliation towards self but through them as tears keeps a heart beating.
Moving with the pace of the earth trying to find the gift that he was
presented with when he was born because he lost it during some time when the sky fell and the stars disappeared from clear vision. He can't find it.

While he is looking, many people delay his search Because of names and titles that are struck upon him. Lashing back at the reason for postponement, he dies somewhere while he had them gasping for air, paddling the hands and feet of partners in an ocean of truth. Resurrected by light he started all over in steel. Rusting his cheeks. Oiled them in unison with his soul that only made one cycle complete. Determined to stretch

REASONS, ROSES, GASES & STEEL (P.3)

his muscles to be one with the truth, he tumbles upon reasons to let go of the rope that binds him rocks he uses to step on to climb. But its to d imple to break. Never resting and never check points and complaining about the things he reall doesn't care about gives him a reason to keep going . Not knowing the things he doesn't know will enable his toes to work up a sweat, to make a point. Running through gardens of shapes of knowledge, he draws his own and marks a path so that it will be a great concrete view for celestrial being's. Things they can't see but are there unified with those who know they are there through actual fact. Brightened with the cool breeze that comes with sunrays in spring, he grabs his body gently and sleeps in divine gases of dreams. Then....

Lights on for the count! he hears.

Mothafuck'n pigs!

FALL

by: JOSE PEREZ

Curiosity got me going towards stair cases of different 1 els. It seems like everything was cleared through understanding. That's good. That's love. Pages strain to leave. So anxious to walk and talk on river rapids. Dismissing ancient actions. Bringing forth infant passages and caves to scream in and raise the way so that it would grow up to be sufficient. Sounds of bells helps my vision. Trying hard to full fill a dream with in a struggle. That type of locker feels locked at this standing point. Because now we pull out our dicks through barb-wire to piss on there ground. We stupid and confused walking with a permanent frown. Flash backs from cups over shells. Bronze under foam. And tall ugly men digging holes next to "here lies John Doe". So now I'm painting pictures so your cause could break through the walls of tall remedy. Keep pen's close to engines when it roars or even laugh or even moan to clone this feeling for tomorrow. But the diamond shattered my dreams It was fake. Now I'm spelling out bones at the casket house in the cemetery.

RUNNING IN LINES
by: JOSE PEREZ

ect when you living a l
kipping through lines
the poem goes
ws

who stool the glimpse to stop foes
and expose those who are molded
most is molded but let me find out
your eye still frozen
Everything seems perfect when you acquired the best part
but you know that a journey
was placed in your eye
for you was a boy who asked why? to why.
never let a bribe grow from toxic water
but water ran through your mind
and you questioned all who slaughtered
and your neck caught a vein
So you engraved your face in cloth so soft
and in came the same thing
different color
Call it weather but different drift
Equipped with tools to make shit seem easy
How could a man-kind declare me crazy
That's crazy!
So everything binds fast when two minds clash to build
and that's just how the poem goes
So I'm running in lines
training this mind never to lie

RUNNING IN LINES (P.2)

but in   all reality I'm hurting inside
         ng to be a better person.
         eave me alone when I travel the globe
with   u   d, one pen and one dome
Speeding and screaming in high notes
Trying to dodge these sweet coats
explode from an annoying tone
because opposites be trying to blame it on you
so you just take those rules
and blame it on you if you fail
because only you could take storms
of snow, rain and hail
trying not to this all over again
then its all over again
sharing pain to a paper and pen

Everything seems perfect when you loving the pain
 nning through lines
 eaning the stains
that clog your heart
So I grip whats close to me
While I listen to my feet stomp loud
and my shoulders shrug.

130

I REMEMBER THAT TIME

by: JOSE PEREZ

To name the diagnosis of my state
probably not engraved in PHD's list
Not what I have
I imagine reality with in a dream
Domestic disputes
regular schemes
untold secrets are held in palms
words that carry beams that burn its target
bull side from the voice that through it
logical praises to my self for
making through tribulation
So prison is a piece of cake
but I want pain
I want it
I need it
Give me more
you see,
I listed myself on the failure list
but I swam through oceans and I ran through desserts
with no water, nobody gave a fuck, I ran
I am. I am survivor. I'm not dead. Not yet.
Waves in pictures threw me off
when it transformed into an alley with dead trees
and a crushed cat on the cars path
but I laughed and I grasped the ghetto's potion
and placed the notion of me being o.k.
but it wasn't. It wasn't

I REMEMBER THAT TIME (P.2)

terns in the sky told me where to go
I could find peace
the skies are never ending.

Imagine   searching behind clouds
and I can't go to neptune to see
                                    not there.
if he or she under there
                              carried me
I was aware of the so-called being
Right into hell when the one that
in his balls decided to come back.
Running that mothafucker tripped me.
I remember that time.

BARB-WIRE NEEDLE PENS

by: JOSE PEREZ

in a corner
Closing othing to keep the grass green
with n
somethi ng ,I'm searching.
Sharp ink roaming in my veins
cutting it deep for a taste
racing to catch a droplet
making a mock of the birds
and pacing fast
to my calendar to mark it
barb-wire wrapped around my body
needle piercing pens
going swiftly through these caves
of a monster.
Blocking, casting, struggling to prosper
Prosper in this fight for humanity
struggling to catch the melody
of this devil
and strangle the demons cuddle
when it tries to love me
The rooms spinning but not me
I see eyes grinning
arms reaching
and ears tilting for a breeze for peace.
Listen,
Fuming in rage
catching the luster of barb-wire
in this cage

BARB-WIRE NEEDLE PENS (P.2)

I refuse to turn this page

  til the light shines

  eply in my cage

The smokes gray.

The smoke clears.

The walls green.

The bloods black.

The most powerful form of a human

is clear in a sea of polluted plants.

DON'T LIE TO ME

by: JOSE PEREZ

Leave it up to the sees of the mind
to wash out the bloody rag
that was thrown at my face by my father
while I was young and wet
I was also dried from love
cause another stranger tried to be my mother
Climbing I was pulled down by the forces of words
that claimed I was there property
I remember the pain that sent chills up my way
and its clarity kills me
Explicit dreams that happened in real life
wakes me up in hot sweat
I don't think that will happen again
but it will come back in a new wrap
Camouflaged with sweet words
but I know it when I see it
Because its bullshit
so don't sugar coat!
I want the whole dose
so that I could know
the highest level of the struggle
that's why I want to be tortured
I want to be brought to the energy
that surrounds your true way
so don't act like its all play
when you're really not good at drama
this is not class, this is real

DON'T LIE TO ME   (P.2)
----

this is what I feel

No love.

No hurt after I realize what it was for

The pain.

So don't tell me that you could stop the rain doctor.

I am sister, brother, mother and mostly,

My own father.

so get the fuck out my face with that shit

fuck ya'll all of ya'll.

AN ANIMAL

by: JOSE PEREZ

I claim I'm shamed
but rain is gained by pain
so hurt is all the same
but its funny how a lame
could burst in flames and hold a torch for fame
and still get forced to tame
an animal
I love this life
I lie but truthfully write
I strive and fight but still I want a light
banged up with pipes
I roam at night and still get cold for rights
but how could you fight an animal
an animal glares at you
spies with cannibal eyes
remain on intangible rides
he dies
an animal
I nag at you
I spit in your face
to them I'm animal
to words I'm wonderful
but to GOD's
I'm POWERFULL

SELF-REALIZATION

"You would know in words that which you have
always known in thought.
You would touch with your fingers
the naked body of your dreams."

Khalil Gibran
(The Prophet [p. 54])

EYES

by: JOSE PEREZ

I witness a lot of things
    selling me dreams
    s claiming I'm King
but I see the opposite
    on on a monster
    m
make sure he doesn't stop crying
I see myself dieing
a life that keeps on lying
an avalanche forms while I'm climbing
I see nothing really
where its supposed to be white at
it's black
    i   posed to be brown at
    r
how it   osed to be open
a sign   your dead
I see nothing
It hurts and burns my eyes
all 3 of them
I see depression
I see deaths button being pressed in darkness
I see throats choking on bones
so eternal there not promised

EYES   (P.2)

I see stars and comets
  see mouths so disgusted they vomit
        moms and pops
     Let me stop it
  only see moms and pops in topics
          plugs in sockets
            going cop it because my body can't grab it
            lot of fucked up ways
I hope that one day
my eyes could peacefully look at my grave
that's after I pay
A VISION.
I see a man of innocence
but guilty of the sin
        uld you do
           ball gets stuck on the rim
              leave it
go home   just think about it
I see people passing by rapidly
girls that want me but can't have me
who dares to laugh at that broken down tree
the branches are rotten
and I can't see a leaf
why not a beam
sunlight shining on a stream

140

EYES   (P.3)

why not   a clear vision but blurry
 og   over the place and dirty
    all
           bound to scream loud around
    ice
         he did and saw
      w the gamble backfires
now 't   law
                      to prepare for war
                      know whats next in store
so he   for a next move
hoping that one day he will get back his groove
I see hell everyday in patterns
I see a lot of shit even birds that scatter
no one bothered them they just flew away
I'll just find another way

                  any movement that's still in the memory
to be blind that means no sign
no way to see time
no way to see sunshine
no predicaments to combine
But I'm glad to see things that are right and wrong
because with out eyes I wouldn't be strong
A VISION

MY LULLABY
by: JOSE PEREZ

The volume grows louder and my shit is filled
could it take more
could it rain any longer
paranoid my eyes look around the song that made this
observes every corner and sees that a brothers in need
my hands reaches to my pockets
and my back lays back at night
so my pupils zoom in to study the light
visions flashes but to fast
am I ready
is my cattle ready for task of another journey
If it is, sing me a song
so this time my decision will be right and exact
but the song already played it's intro.
IT'S READY!
assuming that my body could take more beating's
and I wonder
I wonder if when the wind blows
my cradle would drop
so I lay back in the essence of my cage
and I grip the sides of my head
confused in an illusion that some day I'll fall
I ADMIT
those tears come trickling down my cheek
AND I SOB

MY LULLABY (P.2)

that's my lullaby

that's what you call my song

sweet dreams

until the next hell

THE NEXT STRUGGLE

hold up......

and when those nights go by

the thoughts of my future family is another lullaby

the savage

the wicked dies from tunes of remedy

I want to keep my dreams close to me

form the blueprint for my last mission

My lullaby to survive

sing me my lullaby

I need my lullaby

SO SCREAM!!!

MY 2

By: JOSE PEREZ

Essence of a cage sparks up thoughts correction,
sparks up trillions of thoughts
sounds of savages
what you call my lullaby
the rock of my ranch
my incense
my jazz that mellows my nerves to peace
I do not like the chirp of the bird
nor the snaps of a cricket
definitely not the sound of crunching leaves
I like the taps of the boots
screams of trading
cries of the lonely
and schemes of the abnormal thief

So i sit back and listen
to the lullabies of guys
that place the real deep in their secrets for disguise
I love that legendary 70's story from the ol'timer
or the played out version
of how Mac had this and Rob had that

MY   LULLABY   2 (P.2)

and Tom, Dick and Harry
had sex with her and her
especially at the same time
a different kind of love

There's a time to place that reality
in front of my face
THE FACTS
the black of its nature
my nature
trapped mind that supersedes my intelligence
but just for that long, (that seems like years)
second
questioning destiny
angry at the path in choice
steam from the brain
that made you spill through the air
knocking out hope for a little bit
and glorifying the consequential thought of it
THE WRONG BEHIND THE WRONG
THE WHYS BEHIND THE SCENES
the crushed dreams behind the impulsive move
the pain that co-exist with the past
the supreme being you are

MY LULLABY 2   (P.3)

leads to your boiled knuckles smacking the wall

   sound of my bones cracking

LULLABY

ADVISE
by JOSE PEREZ

* Self correction is done daily when other solutions are triggered through mind scams.
* Improving your way of thinking solves future down falls and could make your person inside stand out more. The real you.
* Rock bottom is hit when your soul can't go the wrong rout no more.
* Your face tingles with pain that hold you back a foot. Your throat fills up with dust bunnies that chokes your neck. Your stomach growls for answers.
* Then every inch in your body charges your pupils and out they come. Those liquefied motrins, the outcome. Confusions.
* Pictures that are drawn by what they said would happen but didn't. I can't believe I only stuck my ear out and thought that this was true.
* But the scene that plays now proves that those was just assumptions. So I'll strive to carry a hidden reason to live.
* So I'll strive and fight to live to find out why my heart must beat another beat. But why no one stopped the leak? But it doesn't matter because I did.
* I tend to think that I must depend on, when I should be making my own rules and making sure I follow my own boundaries. Discipline must bring light to life.
* THEN THE POEM COMES!

THE

By JOSE PEREZ

It always happens like this
I sit here and try to create
a new method
mark my presence
when all I had to do was open my mouth
let my conscious eat at me later

THIS SHIT HURTS SO BAD!

I laugh to hide the state that I'm in
so my person won't shut down
these bad thoughts I leave them in
I am a new person compared to the last time
but now
I have to figure out another way to let go
back in those days
my first few steps upon a path was not controlled
by an angel
I held the hand of a distant stranger
but a distant relative
that began to open up her hand and let me go
so I could walk
and so I walked out of sight

(P.2)

I monkey swung to another hand

that belonged to a stranger

they yanked my arm shoved my body

then another

    pattern for another 10 years

    was a long walk

    do people even care?

MASTER IDENTITY
by: JOSE PEREZ

I hold
   of a a master identity
I kneel shield that covers me
that but it bothers me
     your needle and poison could inject my remedy

A master identity
   allows my shield to cover the real
so you won't draw towards my loop.
Some people kneel and confess,
some people stand and protest
   but nothing's right
could there be anything taller than height

I turn in a form of an right angle
   look to see another world
but for every twist and turn
there is something new to learn
   but how could you avoid that burn

Then everything says it's okay
   and every time your breath comes back
a new law you might want to obey
then that picture gets grafted
in 3-D, so you'll see me

MASTER IDENTITY (P.2)

another man gets drafted
I'm going to put it past me though
FUCK IT

Because I hold that time in my palms
effecting the bomb
to scramble the wrong
then you feel alone in a mist of a song
I BLAME ME!
eyeballs roll up to look at reality
beat a pattern of crime into my humanity
cheat the mountain to climb you hit reality

UNDERSTAND!

because I don't.
    Could you be a man?
because I won't
    I could just pack these words right down my throat
because I wrote my name in the sky
I'm on the list to live with Satan and die
Hop on this ride
I know I'm already in hell
my question is why

MASTER IDENTITY (P.3)

It been why since I was 4
when I had to get a chair to reach
and open the doors
    NOW ITS WAR!
I tell them I don't need no more
I got enough pain and struggles
and rain and troubles
and people think that I lay in puddles
    on purpose
I think I got to open these curtains
    and show you the MASTER IDENTITY
that sparked but never generated
and my anthem is always going to be fuck it

Cause I love to put it past me
    coach this pen to correct me
so I'll teach my soul
and make sure that every chapter unfolds
to give fuel to my heated up coal
    and the fire will expose
MY BONES OF WORDS I TOLD.

Everyday I strive to get to my other half
but the laughs brings forth this task

MASTER IDENTITY   (P.4)

to form a mass of announcements

'm alive until judgment.

   But I don't know why this

but that's it

now I got to used this pen as lips

that opens it's mouth before I boil a fist

Sometimes I think I got to shatter this mirror

   cause my pops was not there

to show me that everything that shines ain't glitter

It ain't gold either

it ain't gold

       and as my own teacher I learned that on my own

So what does that tell you

the title of these words is what I bring you

I hold a,

MASTER IDENTITY.

THANK YOUs!

THANK YOUs

To my Mommy, Guendalina Ruberte, you were the support I needed during the most pivotal moment of my life. Your unwavering strength reminds me of the profound power of connection, even when we long for someone by our side. You have nurtured my spirit and taught me the importance of self-love, showing me that I am deserving of peace and the fulfillment of my dreams. Your belief in me has been a guiding light, and I am forever grateful for the love and wisdom you embody. You gave me the gift of poetry! Rest in Power Mommy!

To Beia Abril Morris Pérez, my daughter, my radiant inspiration, thank you for consistently urging me to move forward! Your presence illuminates my path, and the depth of my love for you is unparalleled. Every moment we share is a treasure, filled with laughter and support. You are my beautiful Pretty Princess, and I cherish the vibrant energy you bring into my life.

To Robin & Ray, your faith in me revealed depths I never knew existed. You nurtured my transformation from boy to man with such grace and understanding. Your thoughtful gestures—whether it was sharing a meal or simply being present—allowed my voice to resonate and grow. Together, we birthed "Future Souls," a testament to our shared journey, and how exhilarating it is to embrace the present! Robin, you were the sole person in my life who was there for me my first few years in Clinton Correctional facility. There were several years were the only letters I received was yours. You were my only connection to the outside world. I am so grateful for that hope you gifted me. The future is indeed now, and I am thankful for the incredible legacy we are building together.

To my beloved siblings—Rebecca, Nelly, Stephanie (Jazzmine), Felipe, Pedro, Mike, Gregory, and Samira—you are forever in my heart. Though distance may separate us, and displaced anger and resentment sometimes govern whether we hang out together. I dream of the day we gather around a table, sharing laughter, love, and memories as a family. Each of you holds a special place in my life, and I look forward to the moments when we can reconnect and celebrate each other once and for all.

To the Nation of Gods and Earths, I am profoundly grateful for your guidance and the divine consciousness you've instilled in me. Your teachings have shaped my understanding of life, affirming that knowledge transforms into wisdom. Thank you for nurturing my spirit and reminding me of my origins, as you collectively elevate the consciousness of our community.

A heartfelt thank you to my teacher, brother, and best friend, Cincere God Allah. Your unwavering dedication has inspired me to seek enlightenment and has equipped me with the tools I need to embrace my identity unapologetically. To my brothers, the Gods—Wise Prophecy Noah Allah, Intelligent Blackman B-Allah, Allah Love Authority, Kassan Supreme Messiah Allah, Supreme Allah (Dupreme), Wise God Allah, and Allah Chosen—your guidance is a cherished gift that I carry with me always.

To my brother, Jason "Jah" Scott (RIP), your memory is forever woven into my heart. I wish you could witness the journey I've taken, but I carry your spirit with me in every step. Your love and support continue to inspire me, and I will love you always, Bro. Rest in Power.

To my brother, my family, my spiritual advisor, and mentor, Dr. Joseph D. Williams, your unwavering support and understanding have been a lifeline in my life. You embody compassion and wisdom, and I am eternally grateful for your presence. You've helped me navigate my path with grace and purpose, and I cherish every lesson you've imparted.

To Rebel, Mr. Taino Domingo, aka TankSinatra, your courage and talent inspire me daily. Thank you for being a consistent force in my life, always uplifting those around you with your powerful voice. I love you forever! We've come a long way from those early days, and I celebrate every moment of growth we've shared.

To my motivator, Larry "Luqman" White (RIP), your honesty and guidance opened doors for me at such a young age. Your influence has been transformative, shaping my understanding of the world and my place within it. Rest in Power, my King; your legacy lives on in all the lives you've touched.

To Rev. Edwin Muller (RIP), your nurturing spirit and profound wisdom made a lasting impact on my life. You taught me the importance of intention and living as a life-giving human being. Your legacy will always guide my path, reminding me to embrace the present and honor the future with purpose.

To Janine Pommy Vega, Rest in Power, my Queen! Your unwavering commitment to the craft of poetry has held me accountable to my art and to myself. Your friendship meant the world to me, and I hope your spirit shines through me as I share my voice with the world. I love you, Jay-9! Your sword was the sharpest!

To Phat Dave and Anthony LaFontant, thank you for connecting me to the Harvest Moon Collective Poetry Group. Your support has been invaluable, creating a space for my voice to flourish and grow. I am deeply grateful for your belief in my work.

To Paul Wellington, my brother, I treasure our bond and look forward to the healing rhythms of our poetry touching many lives. Together, we are stepping into our greatness, and I can't wait to see where our shared journey takes us!

To Father Ford, your gentle lessons have profoundly shaped my understanding of strength. Your wisdom and quiet power remind me that true strength often lies in compassion and humility.

To Rev. Peteru Sebune, thank you for helping me recognize my royal potential. Your insights have empowered me to stand tall and embrace my worth, shaping the leader I aspire to be.

To Mr. Zach Tate, thank you for passing the critical analysis torch. Your transparency and willingness to share your knowledge have illuminated my journey, guiding me toward deeper understanding and growth.

To Anthony Sims, your friendship and mentorship have been pivotal in my growth. Our life-changing conversations have shaped the course of my journey in ways I could never have imagined. I love you, Bro!

To Ronald "Heezie" Hatfield, your authenticity and realness keep our circle strong. I am so proud of the man you've become, and I'm humbled by your sense of self. Though we may have lost a championship, together, we're winning in life! Forty Twooooooo!

To Jason "Jay" Calkins, your unfiltered truth is a gift I deeply appreciate. Thank you for always being real and reminding me of the importance of honesty. To you and Joey Meyers, both of you have vibrant spirits that have enriched my life in so many ways! I'm grateful for the memories, the meals, and the sense of family we've created together.

To Michael "Cino Mike" Flournoy, your quick actions saved me in a critical moment, and I'm grateful for your relentless spirit in our shared struggles. I thank you for how we popped everybody that tried us on the weight court…they can lift all that weight, but they can't do what we do!! That was a lesson I needed that translated to my entire life! I'll never forget! I will always remember how we tackled challenges together, proving that we can lift not only weights but also each other up in life.

To Cub, Mr. Boston, your inspirational attitude continues to motivate me. We've come a long way from our humble beginnings, cooking with nothing but Mrs. Dash and dreaming big! I cherish those memories and look forward to creating even more with you.

To Mr. Rashid, your wisdom and brotherhood are treasures I hold dear. I can't wait to return to ATL and spend time together—next time, let's go out and celebrate our journey!

To Durell "Rel" Smallwood, your leadership and respect taught me invaluable lessons in my youth. You are a legend on and off the court, and your example has inspired countless others to follow their dreams.

To Derrick "Bhar" Stroud, your encouragement to be authentic has empowered me. You taught me perspective and love and attitude and confidence and truth!! You taught me how not to go with what everybody else is going with. It's ok to be different and say Nah, I'm going this way!! Thats being a man. Making your own decisions. Thank you King!

To Wesley Caines, your faith in me gave me my first big break with Maria Davis's showcase at Eastern. I did my thing and the rest is history!!

Thank you Maria Davis for being a bright shining light in our dark world. You didn't have to come inside a prison to bring first class talent to perform for us. Yet you did and also humbled the crowd to let me perform. Thank you!

To Patrick "Dee" Drysdale, your partnership has been a true gift throughout my journey in the Art Tree Theater group. As my scene partner, you have consistently brought an energy and creativity that elevate every performance we share. Whether you were embodying Captain Ahab, inspiring me through the depths of that character, or stepping into the role of Brutus, standing strong by my side, your support has been unwavering. I am deeply grateful for your remarkable talent, brother, and for all the invaluable lessons you've imparted along the way. Your passion for the craft and commitment to excellence inspire me to reach new heights, and I am honored to have you as my lifelong friend and collaborator.

To Charlie Grosso, your leadership within Art Tree Theater has left an indelible mark on my artistic journey. You have a unique ability to create an environment where creativity flourishes and collaboration thrives. The unforgettable memories we've crafted together speak to your dedication and vision, allowing us to explore our potential fully. Your encouragement and belief in our capabilities foster a sense of community that inspires all of us to pursue our passions fearlessly. Thank you for being a guiding light in our artistic endeavors; your impact is truly immeasurable.

To Michael "Mid" Fernandez, your mentorship has profoundly shaped my understanding of strength and humility. You exemplify the power of being soft-spoken while commanding respect and admiration from those around you. Through your guidance, I have learned that true strength lies not in loudness but in quiet confidence and authenticity. Your insights have encouraged me to embrace my own voice and approach life with a gentle spirit. I am grateful for the lessons you've shared and the unwavering support you've provided, which will forever influence my journey. Thank you for being such an integral part of my growth.

To Noah Peoplez, your presence has been a constant source of inspiration in my life. Your peace radiates, creating a calm and uplifting atmosphere wherever you go. Every interaction with you is a masterclass in authenticity; you never hold back, always bringing your full self to every moment. Your talent is not just impressive—it's transformative, and I am eternally grateful for the energy you share with us all.

To Patrick "Kush" Stephens, what an incredible honor it is to call you my friend and brother. You are the intellectual giant who constantly pushes me to think deeper and challenge the status quo. Your dedication to uplifting our youth in the fight against systemic injustices inspires me every day. I am thankful for the bond we share as we strive for change together, and I admire the way you lead with both your mind and your heart.

To Stephen "Green Eyes" Rodriguez (RIP), your vibrant spirit was a beacon of joy in my life. You had the rare ability to celebrate those around you, making each of us feel valued and cherished. I carry your memory with me, and I can almost hear your laughter as I navigate my journey. I hope you're smiling down on me as I pursue my dreams; your light continues to guide me, and I will love you forever.

To Benjamin "Benji" Lozano, our friendship has blossomed into a bond that feels unbreakable. You are the one I want by my side when it's time to celebrate life, and I truly cherish the moments we share with our brother Cuzo. Having you in my life has brought me immense joy and reassurance; it feels like we can conquer anything together. Thank you for being the steadfast friend I can always count on.

To Jose "Plus" Pineda, you have been my rock since my return home. Your unwavering support and friendship have been invaluable, providing me with strength when I needed it most. I am grateful for the paths we've walked together and the memories we've created. Your presence in my life gave me a sense of belonging, and I honor you as a true king.

To Javier Miranda, we've navigated countless struggles together, sharing both challenges and triumphs. The bond we've formed through our shared experiences is something I deeply treasure. Having eaten the same bread, we've built a foundation of mutual respect and understanding. It is an honor to stand beside you as a brother and fellow leader in our work.

To Anthony "Bam" Perez, your authenticity is a breath of fresh air in a world that can often feel superficial. I am thankful for your friendship and the warmth that you and your family bring into my life. Your humility and intelligence are qualities that inspire me to strive for greatness in everything I do. Thank you for being one of the most genuine people I know!

To John Adrian Valasquez, you quickly became family, and our connection feels like a meeting of kindred souls. Witnessing your journey to exoneration fills me with joy, and I am grateful for the friendship we've cultivated along the way. Now that you're out, let's roll up our sleeves and get to work! We have so much to accomplish together, and I can't wait to see where our shared path leads us.

To Dan Seplian, my brother, I am grateful to have you by my side as we tackle the challenges ahead. Your strength and dedication make you a champion in our community, and I am constantly inspired by your greatness. Together, we have a mission to fulfill, and I will always stand beside you in the fight. Let's go!

To the Rehabilitation Through the Arts program, your transformative impact on lives is immeasurable. You have given many individuals the tools to express themselves and heal through creativity, reshaping futures and igniting hope. I am thankful for the opportunities you provide and the positive changes you inspire in so many.

To Katherine Vockins, the founder of the RTA program, your light has illuminated the darkest corners for many of us. Your vision and commitment have created a nurturing environment where creativity flourishes, and I am profoundly grateful for your leadership. You are a guiding star in our community, and your influence continues to inspire us all.

To Charles Moore, your ability to keep us on our toes is a gift. You are the thoughtful partner we all need, challenging us to think critically and engage deeply with our work. Your dedication to community and collaboration inspires growth in everyone around you, and I am thankful for the partnership we share.

To Max Kenner, thank you for believing in me during my journey to Bard. Your willingness to see beyond the surface and recognize my potential means more to me than words can express. I am humbled and grateful for your support, which helped pave the way for my educational journey.

To the Bard Prison Initiative, your commitment to education and empowerment has changed countless lives. Your work fosters hope and resilience in the face of adversity, and I am proud to be part of a community that values knowledge and transformation.

To the Men of Exodus (1968-2020), your legacy inspires us all to push forward. The paths you forged for future generations of leaders are invaluable, and I honor the sacrifices you made to create a better world for those who follow.

To the Harvest Moon Collective, your artistry and dedication bring our community together in celebration of creativity and expression. The collective spirit you foster is a testament to the power of collaboration, and I am grateful to be part of this vibrant network.

To the Art Tree Theater Group, thank you for your unwavering commitment to the arts. Your work not only entertains but also educates and empowers those involved, creating a space for growth and connection. I appreciate the joy and healing your performances bring.

To the Alternatives to Violence Project Men, your dedication to fostering peace and understanding in our community is commendable. The work you do transforms lives and creates a ripple effect of positivity that extends far beyond your immediate circle.

To Puppies Behind Bars, Inc., your compassion and commitment to rehabilitation through the bond of animals is truly inspiring. You demonstrate that love and support can take many forms, and I am grateful for the impact you make in the lives of both humans and dogs.

To Hudson Link, your support in bridging education and reintegration has been transformative for so many. I appreciate the opportunities you provide to empower individuals to thrive after incarceration.

To the New York Theological Seminary (North Campus), thank you for fostering a space of learning and growth. Your commitment to educating future leaders is invaluable, and I am grateful for the experiences I've had within your walls.

To Maria Caba, I cannot thank you enough for being the catalyst that opened my heart to share my story on my own terms. Your unwavering support has encouraged me to embrace my true self and love who I am unconditionally. Through your compassionate guidance, you helped me realize that I am deserving of love, peace, and the pursuit of my dreams, no matter where they may lead. Your ability to see me for who I truly am has not only empowered me but has also inspired me to honor my own journey. I am profoundly grateful for the wisdom you've imparted and the love you've shared; you've truly helped change my life and I cherish our friendship.

To Julia Davis, you are my rock in both my professional and personal life. Your steadfast friendship has been a source of strength as we navigate the complexities of our work together. You have welcomed me into your world, where we fight for the most vulnerable among us, and together, we are creating powerful paradigm shifts that uplift not only my former teenage self but countless other children from foster care. Your passion and determination make you one of the most powerful people in my life, and I am proud to call you my partner in this fight. We truly are the heavyweight tag team champions of child welfare, and I couldn't ask for a better ally.

To Elpetha Tsivicos, co-founder of One Whales Tale who gave me my first acting gig as

Solomon in Quince. I want to take a moment to express my heartfelt gratitude for everything you've brought into my life. Your kindness and respect have created a safe space where I can truly be myself. You see me for who I am, not for my past, and that is a rare gift. Your passion for sharing your favorite things with others speaks volumes about your generous spirit. You embody hope in every interaction, (her name means Hope!) inspiring those around you to dream big. You dream with a fire that pulls others in, and that energy is contagious! I've learned so much from your encouragement, and I am thrilled to be a part of this journey as a collaborating artist. I can't wait to see what the future holds for us at One Whales Tale Theater Company!

To Camilo Quirez-Vazquez, I am incredibly thankful for the joy and opportunities you've shared with me through our friendship. Your support as a co-founder of One Whales Tale Theater Company with Elpetha has allowed me to showcase my art in ways I never thought possible. Your respect and honor for everyone around you make it easy to feel valued and inspired. I love how you become my brother and share your passions without hesitation; it truly shows your generous heart. I am excited to collaborate as an artist and look forward to our shared journey ahead. Thank you for being such a bright light in my life!

If I spelled your name wrong, or if I spelled your attribute wrong, I sincerely apologize. If I've missed anyone's name, please accept my heartfelt apologies. I am humbled by this moment and the many influences that have shaped my journey. I promise to honor you all by continuing to be ME. Take care of yourself!

"Till Ink Meets Paper"

Love, Jose A. Perez

COMING SOON
More titles by Jose A. Perez

Colorful Shards of Mirror: Poems & Rhythms
Spring 2025

The Walls of A Gray Cloud:
Poems by a Teenage Lifer
Spring 2025

Give Me the Words: A Foster Boy's Memoir
Fall 2025

Follow me on:
Instagram
@j.a._perezz
@healingrhythms_poetry

Facebook
@Jose Angel Perez

X
@thereel_JAperez

TikTok
@j.a.perezz

LinkedIn
@Jose Perez

'Till Ink Meets Paper

POEMS FOR GUENDALINA...
MY MOMMY

www.ingramcontent.com/pod-product-compliance
Lightning Source LLC
Chambersburg PA
CBHW071206160426
43196CB00011B/2210